The Bride of Abydos by Lord Byron

A TURKISH TALE

George Gordon Byron, 6th Baron Byron, but more commonly known as just Byron was a leading English poet in the Romantic Movement along with Keats and Shelley.

Byron was born on January 22nd, 1788. He was a great traveller across Europe, spending many years in Italy and much time in Greece. With his aristocratic indulgences, flamboyant style along with his debts, and a string of lovers he was the constant talk of society.

In 1823 he joined the Greeks in their war of Independence against the Ottoman Empire, both helping to fund and advise on the war's conduct.

It was an extraordinary adventure, even by his own standards. But, for us, it is his poetry for which he is mainly remembered even though it is difficult to see where he had time to write his works of immense beauty. But write them he did.

He died on April 19th 1824 after having contracted a cold which, on the advice of his doctors, was treated with blood-letting. This cause complications and a violent fever set in. Byron died like his fellow romantics, tragically young and on some foreign field.

"Had we never loved sae kindly,
Had we never loved sae blindly,
Never met—or never parted,
We had ne'er been broken-hearted."—
Burns - Farewell to Nancy.

Index of Contents
INTRODUCTION TO THE BRIDE OF ABYDOS
DEDICATION
CANTO THE FIRST
CANTO THE SECOND
NOTE TO THE MSS. OF THE BRIDE OF ABYDOS
REVISES
LORD BYRON – A SHORT BIOGRAPHY
LORD BYRON – A CONCISE BIBLIOGRAPHY

INTRODUCTION TO THE BRIDE OF ABYDOS

Many poets—Wordsworth, for instance—have been conscious in their old age that an interest attaches to the circumstances of the composition of their poems, and have furnished their friends and admirers with explanatory notes. Byron recorded the motif and occasion of the Bride of Abydos while the poem was still in the press. It was written, he says, to divert his mind, "to wring his thoughts from reality to imagination—from selfish regrets to vivid recollections" (Diary, December 5,

1813, Letters, ii. 361), "to distract his dreams from ..." (Diary, November 16) "for the sake of employment" (Letter to Moore, November 30, 1813). He had been staying during part of October and November at Aston Hall, Rotherham, with his friend James Wedderburn Webster, and had fallen in love with his friend's wife, Lady Frances. From a brief note to his sister, dated November 5, we learn that he was in a scrape, but in "no immediate peril," and from the lines, "Remember him, whom Passion's power" (vide ante, p. 67), we may infer that he had sought safety in flight. The Bride of Abydos, or Zuleika, as it was first entitled, was written early in November, "in four nights" (Diary, November 16), or in a week (Letter to Gifford, November 12)—the reckoning goes for little—as a counter-irritant to the pain and distress of amour interrompu.

The confession or apology is eminently characteristic. Whilst the Giaour was still in process of evolution, still "lengthening its rattles," another Turkish poem is offered to the public, and the natural explanation, that the author is in vein, and can score another trick, is felt to be inadequate and dishonouring—"To withdraw myself from myself," he confides to his Diary (November 27), "has ever been my sole, my entire, my sincere motive for scribbling at all."

It is more than probable that in his twenty-sixth year Byron had not attained to perfect self-knowledge, but there is no reason to question his sincerity. That Byron loved to surround himself with mystery, and to dissociate himself from "the general," is true enough; but it does not follow that at all times and under all circumstances he was insincere. "Once a poseur always a poseur" is a rough-and-ready formula not invariably applicable even to a poet.

But the Bride of Abydos was a tonic as well as a styptic. Like the Giaour, it embodied a personal experience, and recalled "a country replete with the darkest and brightest, but always the most lively colours of my memory" (Diary, December 5, 1813).

In a letter to Galt (December 11, 1813, Letters, 1898, ii. 304, reprinted from Life of Byron, pp. 181, 182) Byron maintains that the first part of the Bride was drawn from "observations" of his own, "from existence." He had, it would appear, intended to make the story turn on the guilty love of a brother for a sister, a tragic incident of life in a Harem, which had come under his notice during his travels in the East, but "on second thoughts" had reflected that he lived "two centuries at least too late for the subject," and that not even the authority of the "finest works of the Greeks," or of Schiller (in the Bride of Messina), or of Alfieri (in Mirra), "in modern times," would sanction the intrusion of the μισητὸν [misêto] into English literature. The early drafts and variants of the MS. do not afford any evidence of this alteration of the plot which, as Byron thought, was detrimental to the poem as a work of art, but the undoubted fact that the Bride of Abydos, as well as the Giaour, embody recollections of actual scenes and incidents which had burnt themselves into the memory of an eye-witness, accounts not only for the fervent heat at which these Turkish tales were written, but for the extraordinary glamour which they threw over contemporary readers, to whom the local colouring was new and attractive, and who were not out of conceit with "good Monsieur Melancholy."

Byron was less dissatisfied with his second Turkish tale than he had been with the Giaour. He apologizes for the rapidity with which it had been composed—stans pede in uno—but he announced to Murray (November 20) that "he was doing his best to beat the Giaour," and (November 29) he appraises the Bride as "my first entire composition of any length."

Moreover, he records (November 15), with evident gratification, the approval of his friend Hodgson, "a very sincere and by no means (at times) a flattering critic of mine," and modestly accepts the praise of such masters of letters as "Mr. Canning," Hookham Frere, Heber, Lord Holland, and of the traveller Edward Daniel Clarke.

The Bride of Abydos was advertised in the Morning Chronicle, among "Books published this day," on November 29, 1813. It was reviewed by George Agar Ellis in the Quarterly Review of January, 1814 (vol. x. p. 331), and, together with the Corsair, by Jeffrey in the Edinburgh Review of April, 1814 (vol. xxiii. p. 198).

DEDICATION

To the right honourable LORD HOLLAND, this tale is inscribed, with every sentiment of regard and respect, by his gratefully obliged and sincere friend,
BYRON.

THE BRIDE OF ABYDOS

CANTO THE FIRST

I.

Know ye the land where the cypress and myrtle
Are emblems of deeds that are done in their clime?
Where the rage of the vulture, the love of the turtle,
Now melt into sorrow, now madden to crime?
Know ye the land of the cedar and vine,
Where the flowers ever blossom, the beams ever shine;
Where the light wings of Zephyr, oppressed with perfume,
Wax faint o'er the gardens of Gúl in her bloom;
Where the citron and olive are fairest of fruit,
And the voice of the nightingale never is mute;
Where the tints of the earth, and the hues of the sky,
In colour though varied, in beauty may vie,
And the purple of Ocean is deepest in dye;
Where the virgins are soft as the roses they twine,
And all, save the spirit of man, is divine—
Tis the clime of the East—'tis the land of the Sun—
Can he smile on such deeds as his children have done?
Oh! wild as the accents of lovers' farewell
Are the hearts which they bear, and the tales which they tell.

II.

Begirt with many a gallant slave,
Apparelled as becomes the brave,
Awaiting each his Lord's behest
To guide his steps, or guard his rest,

Old Giaffir sate in his Divan:
Deep thought was in his agéd eye;
And though the face of Mussulman
Not oft betrays to standers by
The mind within, well skilled to hide
All but unconquerable pride,
His pensive cheek and pondering brow
Did more than he was wont avow.

III.

"Let the chamber be cleared."—The train disappeared—
"Now call me the chief of the Haram guard"—
With Giaffir is none but his only son,
And the Nubian awaiting the sire's award.
"Haroun—when all the crowd that wait
Are passed beyond the outer gate,
(Woe to the head whose eye beheld
My child Zuleika's face unveiled!)
Hence, lead my daughter from her tower—
Her fate is fixed this very hour;
Yet not to her repeat my thought—
By me alone be duty taught!"

"Pacha! to hear is to obey."—
No more must slave to despot say—
Then to the tower had ta'en his way:
But here young Selim silence brake,
First lowly rendering reverence meet;
And downcast looked, and gently spake,
Still standing at the Pacha's feet:
For son of Moslem must expire,
Ere dare to sit before his sire!
"Father! for fear that thou shouldst chide
My sister, or her sable guide—
Know—for the fault, if fault there be,
Was mine—then fall thy frowns on me!
So lovelily the morning shone,
That—let the old and weary sleep—
I could not; and to view alone
The fairest scenes of land and deep,
With none to listen and reply
To thoughts with which my heart beat high
Were irksome—for whate'er my mood,
In sooth I love not solitude;
I on Zuleika's slumber broke,
And, as thou knowest that for me
Soon turns the Haram's grating key,
Before the guardian slaves awoke
We to the cypress groves had flown,

And made earth, main, and heaven our own!
There lingered we, beguiled too long
With Mejnoun's tale, or Sadi's song;
Till I, who heard the deep tambour
Beat thy Divan's approaching hour,
To thee, and to my duty true,
Warned by the sound, to greet thee flew:
But there Zuleika wanders yet—
Nay, Father, rage not—nor forget
That none can pierce that secret bower
But those who watch the women's tower."

IV.

"Son of a slave"—the Pacha said—
"From unbelieving mother bred,
Vain were a father's hope to see
Aught that beseems a man in thee.
Thou, when thine arm should bend the bow,
And hurl the dart, and curb the steed,
Thou, Greek in soul if not in creed,
Must pore where babbling waters flow,
And watch unfolding roses blow.
Would that yon Orb, whose matin glow
Thy listless eyes so much admire,
Would lend thee something of his fire!
Thou, who woulds't see this battlement
By Christian cannon piecemeal rent;
Nay, tamely view old Stambol's wall
Before the dogs of Moscow fall,
Nor strike one stroke for life and death
Against the curs of Nazareth!
Go—let thy less than woman's hand
Assume the distaff—not the brand.
But, Haroun!—to my daughter speed:
And hark—of thine own head take heed—
If thus Zuleika oft takes wing—
Thou see'st yon bow—it hath a string!"

V.

No sound from Selim's lip was heard,
At least that met old Giaffir's ear,
But every frown and every word
Pierced keener than a Christian's sword.
"Son of a slave!—reproached with fear!
Those gibes had cost another dear.
Son of a slave!—and who my Sire?"
Thus held his thoughts their dark career;

And glances ev'n of more than ire
Flash forth, then faintly disappear.
Old Giaffir gazed upon his son
And started; for within his eye
He read how much his wrath had done;
He saw rebellion there begun:
"Come hither, boy—what, no reply?
I mark thee—and I know thee too;
But there be deeds thou dar'st not do:
But if thy beard had manlier length,
And if thy hand had skill and strength,
I'd joy to see thee break a lance,
Albeit against my own perchance."
As sneeringly these accents fell,
On Selim's eye he fiercely gazed:
That eye returned him glance for glance,
And proudly to his Sire's was raised,
Till Giaffir's quailed and shrunk askance—
And why—he felt, but durst not tell.
"Much I misdoubt this wayward boy
Will one day work me more annoy:
I never loved him from his birth,
And—but his arm is little worth,
And scarcely in the chase could cope
With timid fawn or antelope,
Far less would venture into strife
Where man contends for fame and life—
I would not trust that look or tone:
No—nor the blood so near my own.
That blood—he hath not heard—no more—
I'll watch him closer than before.
He is an Arab to my sight,
Or Christian crouching in the fight—
But hark!—I hear Zuleika's voice;
Like Houris' hymn it meets mine ear:
She is the offspring of my choice;
Oh! more than ev'n her mother dear,
With all to hope, and nought to fear—
My Peri! ever welcome here!
Sweet, as the desert fountain's wave
To lips just cooled in time to save—
Such to my longing sight art thou;
Nor can they waft to Mecca's shrine
More thanks for life, than I for thine,
Who blest thy birth and bless thee now."

VI.

Fair, as the first that fell of womankind,
When on that dread yet lovely serpent smiling,

Whose Image then was stamped upon her mind—
But once beguiled—and ever more beguiling;
Dazzling, as that, oh! too transcendent vision
To Sorrow's phantom-peopled slumber given,
When heart meets heart again in dreams Elysian,
And paints the lost on Earth revived in Heaven;
Soft, as the memory of buried love;
Pure, as the prayer which Childhood wafts above;
Was she—the daughter of that rude old Chief,
Who met the maid with tears—but not of grief.

Who hath not proved how feebly words essay
To fix one spark of Beauty's heavenly ray?
Who doth not feel, until his failing sight
Faints into dimness with its own delight,
His changing cheek, his sinking heart confess
The might—the majesty of Loveliness?
Such was Zuleika—such around her shone
The nameless charms unmarked by her alone—
The light of Love, the purity of Grace,
The mind, the Music breathing from her face,
The heart whose softness harmonized the whole,
And oh! that eye was in itself a Soul!

Her graceful arms in meekness bending
Across her gently-budding breast;
At one kind word those arms extending
To clasp the neck of him who blest
His child caressing and carest,
Zuleika came—and Giaffir felt
His purpose half within him melt:
Not that against her fancied weal
His heart though stern could ever feel;
Affection chained her to that heart;
Ambition tore the links apart.

VII.

"Zuleika! child of Gentleness!
How dear this very day must tell,
When I forget my own distress,
In losing what I love so well,
To bid thee with another dwell:
Another! and a braver man
Was never seen in battle's van.
We Moslem reck not much of blood:
But yet the line of Carasman
Unchanged, unchangeable hath stood
First of the bold Timariot bands
That won and well can keep their lands.

Enough that he who comes to woo
Is kinsman of the Bey Oglou:
His years need scarce a thought employ;
I would not have thee wed a boy.
And thou shalt have a noble dower:
And his and my united power
Will laugh to scorn the death-firman,
Which others tremble but to scan,
And teach the messenger what fate
The bearer of such boon may wait.
And now thou know'st thy father's will;
All that thy sex hath need to know:
'Twas mine to teach obedience still—
The way to love, thy Lord may show."

VIII.

In silence bowed the virgin's head;
And if her eye was filled with tears
That stifled feeling dare not shed,
And changed her cheek from pale to red,
And red to pale, as through her ears
Those wingéd words like arrows sped,
What could such be but maiden fears?
So bright the tear in Beauty's eye,
Love half regrets to kiss it dry;
So sweet the blush of Bashfulness,
Even Pity scarce can wish it less!

Whate'er it was the sire forgot:
Or if remembered, marked it not;
Thrice clapped his hands, and called his steed,
Resigned his gem-adorned chibouque,
And mounting featly for the mead,
With Maugrabee1 and Mamaluke,
His way amid his Delis took,
To witness many an active deed
With sabre keen, or blunt jerreed.
The Kislar only and his Moors
Watch well the Haram's massy doors.

IX.

His head was leant upon his hand,
His eye looked o'er the dark blue water
That swiftly glides and gently swells
Between the winding Dardanelles;
But yet he saw nor sea nor strand,
Nor even his Pacha's turbaned band

Mix in the game of mimic slaughter,
Careering cleave the folded felt
With sabre stroke right sharply dealt;
Nor marked the javelin-darting crowd,
Nor heard their Ollahs wild and loud—
He thought but of old Giaffir's daughter!

X.

No word from Selim's bosom broke;
One sigh Zuleika's thought bespoke:
Still gazed he through the lattice grate,
Pale, mute, and mournfully sedate.
To him Zuleika's eye was turned,
But little from his aspect learned:
Equal her grief, yet not the same;
Her heart confessed a gentler flame:
But yet that heart, alarmed or weak,
She knew not why, forbade to speak.
Yet speak she must—but when essay?
"How strange he thus should turn away!
Not thus we e'er before have met;
Not thus shall be our parting yet."
Thrice paced she slowly through the room,
And watched his eye—it still was fixed:
She snatched the urn wherein was mixed
The Persian Atar-gul's perfume,
And sprinkled all its odours o'er
The pictured roof and marble floor:
The drops, that through his glittering vest
The playful girl's appeal addressed,
Unheeded o'er his bosom flew,
As if that breast were marble too.
"What, sullen yet? it must not be—
Oh! gentle Selim, this from thee!"
She saw in curious order set
The fairest flowers of Eastern land—
"He loved them once; may touch them yet,
If offered by Zuleika's hand."
The childish thought was hardly breathed
Before the rose was plucked and wreathed;
The next fond moment saw her seat
Her fairy form at Selim's feet:
"This rose to calm my brother's cares
A message from the Bulbul bears;
It says to-night he will prolong
For Selim's ear his sweetest song;
And though his note is somewhat sad,
He'll try for once a strain more glad,
With some faint hope his altered lay

May sing these gloomy thoughts away.

XI.

"What! not receive my foolish flower?
Nay then I am indeed unblest:
On me can thus thy forehead lower?
And know'st thou not who loves thee best?
Oh, Selim dear! oh, more than dearest!
Say, is it me thou hat'st or fearest?
Come, lay thy head upon my breast,
And I will kiss thee into rest,
Since words of mine, and songs must fail,
Ev'n from my fabled nightingale.
I knew our sire at times was stern,
But this from thee had yet to learn:
Too well I know he loves thee not;
But is Zuleika's love forgot?
Ah! deem I right? the Pacha's plan—
This kinsman Bey of Carasman
Perhaps may prove some foe of thine.
If so, I swear by Mecca's shrine,—
If shrines that ne'er approach allow
To woman's step admit her vow,—
Without thy free consent—command—
The Sultan should not have my hand!
Think'st thou that I could bear to part
With thee, and learn to halve my heart?
Ah! were I severed from thy side,
Where were thy friend—and who my guide?
Years have not seen, Time shall not see,
The hour that tears my soul from thee:
Ev'n Azrael, from his deadly quiver
When flies that shaft, and fly it must,
That parts all else, shall doom for ever
Our hearts to undivided dust!"

XII.

He lived—he breathed—he moved—he felt;
He raised the maid from where she knelt;
His trance was gone, his keen eye shone
With thoughts that long in darkness dwelt;
With thoughts that burn—in rays that melt.
As the stream late concealed
By the fringe of its willows,
When it rushes reveal'd
In the light of its billows;
As the bolt bursts on high

From the black cloud that bound it,
Flashed the soul of that eye
Through the long lashes round it.
A war-horse at the trumpet's sound,
A lion roused by heedless hound,
A tyrant waked to sudden strife
By graze of ill-directed knife,
Starts not to more convulsive life
Than he, who heard that vow, displayed,
And all, before repressed, betrayed:
"Now thou art mine, for ever mine,
With life to keep, and scarce with life resign;
Now thou art mine, that sacred oath,
Though sworn by one, hath bound us both.
Yes, fondly, wisely hast thou done;
That vow hath saved more heads than one:
But blench not thou—thy simplest tress
Claims more from me than tenderness;
I would not wrong the slenderest hair
That clusters round thy forehead fair,
For all the treasures buried far
Within the caves of Istakar.
This morning clouds upon me lowered,
Reproaches on my head were showered,
And Giaffir almost called me coward!
Now I have motive to be brave;
The son of his neglected slave,
Nay, start not,'twas the term he gave,
May show, though little apt to vaunt,
A heart his words nor deeds can daunt.
His son, indeed!—yet, thanks to thee,
Perchance I am, at least shall be;
But let our plighted secret vow
Be only known to us as now.
I know the wretch who dares demand
From Giaffir thy reluctant hand;
More ill-got wealth, a meaner soul
Holds not a Musselim's control;
Was he not bred in Egripo?
A viler race let Israel show!
But let that pass—to none be told
Our oath; the rest shall time unfold.
To me and mine leave Osman Bey!
I've partisans for Peril's day:
Think not I am what I appear;
I've arms—and friends—and vengeance near."

XIII.

"Think not thou art what thou appearest!

My Selim, thou art sadly changed:
This morn I saw thee gentlest—dearest—
But now thou'rt from thyself estranged.
My love thou surely knew'st before,
It ne'er was less—nor can be more.
To see thee—hear thee—near thee stay—
And hate the night—I know not why,
Save that we meet not but by day;
With thee to live, with thee to die,
I dare not to my hope deny:
Thy cheek—thine eyes—thy lips to kiss—
Like this—and this—no more than this;
For, Allah! sure thy lips are flame:
What fever in thy veins is flushing?
My own have nearly caught the same,
At least I feel my cheek, too, blushing.
To soothe thy sickness, watch thy health,
Partake, but never waste thy wealth,
Or stand with smiles unmurmuring by,
And lighten half thy poverty;
Do all but close thy dying eye,
For that I could not live to try;
To these alone my thoughts aspire:
More can I do? or thou require?
But, Selim, thou must answer why
We need so much of mystery?
The cause I cannot dream nor tell,
But be it, since thou say'st 'tis well;
Yet what thou mean'st by 'arms' and 'friends,'
Beyond my weaker sense extends.
I meant that Giaffir should have heard
The very vow I plighted thee;
His wrath would not revoke my word:
But surely he would leave me free.
Can this fond wish seem strange in me,
To be what I have ever been?
What other hath Zuleika seen
From simple childhood's earliest hour?
What other can she seek to see
Than thee, companion of her bower,
The partner of her infancy?
These cherished thoughts with life begun,
Say, why must I no more avow?
What change is wrought to make me shun
The truth—my pride, and thine till now?
To meet the gaze of stranger's eyes
Our law—our creed—our God denies;
Nor shall one wandering thought of mine
At such, our Prophet's will, repine:
No! happier made by that decree,
He left me all in leaving thee.

Deep were my anguish, thus compelled
To wed with one I ne'er beheld:
This wherefore should I not reveal?
Why wilt thou urge me to conceal?
I know the Pacha's haughty mood
To thee hath never boded good;
And he so often storms at nought,
Allah! forbid that e'er he ought!
And why I know not, but within
My heart concealment weighs like sin.
If then such secrecy be crime,
And such it feels while lurking here;
Oh, Selim! tell me yet in time,
Nor leave me thus to thoughts of fear.
Ah! yonder see the Tchocadar,
My father leaves the mimic war;
I tremble now to meet his eye—
Say, Selim, canst thou tell me why?"

XIV.

"Zuleika—to thy tower's retreat
Betake thee—Giaffir I can greet:
And now with him I fain must prate
Of firmans, imposts, levies, state.
There's fearful news from Danube's banks,
Our Vizier nobly thins his ranks
For which the Giaour may give him thanks!
Our Sultan hath a shorter way
Such costly triumph to repay.
But, mark me, when the twilight drum
Hath warned the troops to food and sleep,
Unto thy cell with Selim come;
Then softly from the Haram creep
Where we may wander by the deep:
Our garden battlements are steep;
Nor these will rash intruder climb
To list our words, or stint our time;
And if he doth, I want not steel
Which some have felt, and more may feel.
Then shalt thou learn of Selim more
Than thou hast heard or thought before:
Trust me, Zuleika—fear not me!
Thou know'st I hold a Haram key."

"Fear thee, my Selim! ne'er till now
Did words like this—"

"Delay not thou;
I keep the key—and Haroun's guard

Have some, and hope of more reward.
To-night, Zuleika, thou shalt hear
My tale, my purpose, and my fear:
I am not, love! what I appear."

CANTO THE SECOND.

I.

The winds are high on Helle's wave,
As on that night of stormy water
When Love, who sent, forgot to save
The young—the beautiful—the brave—
The lonely hope of Sestos' daughter.
Oh! when alone along the sky
Her turret-torch was blazing high,
Though rising gale, and breaking foam,
And shrieking sea-birds warned him home;
And clouds aloft and tides below,
With signs and sounds, forbade to go,
He could not see, he would not hear,
Or sound or sign foreboding fear;
His eye but saw that light of Love,
The only star it hailed above;
His ear but rang with Hero's song,
"Ye waves, divide not lovers long!"—
That tale is old, but Love anew
May nerve young hearts to prove as true.

II.

The winds are high and Helle's tide
Rolls darkly heaving to the main;
And Night's descending shadows hide
That field with blood bedewed in vain,
The desert of old Priam's pride;
The tombs, sole relics of his reign,
All—save immortal dreams that could beguile
The blind old man of Scio's rocky isle!

III.

Oh! yet—for there my steps have been;
These feet have pressed the sacred shore,
These limbs that buoyant wave hath borne—
Minstrel! with thee to muse, to mourn,
To trace again those fields of yore,

Believing every hillock green
Contains no fabled hero's ashes,
And that around the undoubted scene
Thine own "broad Hellespont" still dashes,
Be long my lot! and cold were he
Who there could gaze denying thee!

IV.

The Night hath closed on Helle's stream,
Nor yet hath risen on Ida's hill
That Moon, which shone on his high theme:
No warrior chides her peaceful beam,
But conscious shepherds bless it still.
Their flocks are grazing on the Mound
Of him who felt the Dardan's arrow:
That mighty heap of gathered ground
Which Ammon's son ran proudly round,
By nations raised, by monarchs crowned,
Is now a lone and nameless barrow!
Within—thy dwelling-place how narrow!
Without—can only strangers breathe
The name of him that was beneath:
Dust long outlasts the storied stone;
But Thou—thy very dust is gone!

V.

Late, late to-night will Dian cheer
The swain, and chase the boatman's fear;
Till then—no beacon on the cliff
May shape the course of struggling skiff;
The scattered lights that skirt the bay,
All, one by one, have died away;
The only lamp of this lone hour
Is glimmering in Zuleika's tower.
Yes! there is light in that lone chamber,
And o'er her silken ottoman
Are thrown the fragrant beads of amber,
O'er which her fairy fingers ran;
Near these, with emerald rays beset,
(How could she thus that gem forget?)
Her mother's sainted amulet,
Whereon engraved the Koorsee text,
Could smooth this life, and win the next;
And by her Comboloio lies
A Koran of illumined dyes;
And many a bright emblazoned rhyme
By Persian scribes redeemed from Time;

And o'er those scrolls, not oft so mute,
Reclines her now neglected lute;
And round her lamp of fretted gold
Bloom flowers in urns of China's mould;
The richest work of Iran's loom,
And Sheeraz tribute of perfume;

All that can eye or sense delight
Are gathered in that gorgeous room:
But yet it hath an air of gloom.
She, of this Peri cell the sprite,
What doth she hence, and on so rude a night?

VI.

Wrapt in the darkest sable vest,
Which none save noblest Moslem wear,
To guard from winds of Heaven the breast
As Heaven itself to Selim dear,
With cautious steps the thicket threading,
And starting oft, as through the glade
The gust its hollow moanings made,
Till on the smoother pathway treading,
More free her timid bosom beat,
The maid pursued her silent guide;
And though her terror urged retreat,
How could she quit her Selim's side?
How teach her tender lips to chide?

VII.

They reached at length a grotto, hewn
By nature, but enlarged by art,
Where oft her lute she wont to tune,
And oft her Koran conned apart;
And oft in youthful reverie
She dreamed what Paradise might be:
Where Woman's parted soul shall go
Her Prophet had disdained to show;
But Selim's mansion was secure,
Nor deemed she, could he long endure
His bower in other worlds of bliss
Without her, most beloved in this!
Oh! who so dear with him could dwell?
What Houri soothe him half so well?

VIII.

Since last she visited the spot
Some change seemed wrought within the grot:
It might be only that the night
Disguised things seen by better light:
That brazen lamp but dimly threw
A ray of no celestial hue;
But in a nook within the cell
Her eye on stranger objects fell.
There arms were piled, not such as wield
The turbaned Delis in the field;
But brands of foreign blade and hilt,
And one was red—perchance with guilt!
Ah! how without can blood be spilt?
A cup too on the board was set
That did not seem to hold sherbet.
What may this mean? she turned to see
Her Selim—"Oh! can this be he?"

IX.

His robe of pride was thrown aside,
His brow no high-crowned turban bore,
But in its stead a shawl of red,
Wreathed lightly round, his temples wore:
That dagger, on whose hilt the gem
Were worthy of a diadem,
No longer glittered at his waist,
Where pistols unadorned were braced;
And from his belt a sabre swung,
And from his shoulder loosely hung
The cloak of white, the thin capote
That decks the wandering Candiote;
Beneath—his golden plated vest
Clung like a cuirass to his breast;
The greaves below his knee that wound
With silvery scales were sheathed and bound.
But were it not that high command
Spake in his eye, and tone, and hand,
All that a careless eye could see
In him was some young Galiongée.

X.

"I said I was not what I seemed;
And now thou see'st my words were true:
I have a tale thou hast not dreamed,
If sooth—its truth must others rue.
My story now 'twere vain to hide,
I must not see thee Osman's bride:

But had not thine own lips declared
How much of that young heart I shared,
I could not, must not, yet have shown
The darker secret of my own.
In this I speak not now of love;
That—let Time—Truth—and Peril prove:
But first—Oh! never wed another—
Zuleika! I am not thy brother!"

XI.

"Oh! not my brother!—yet unsay—
God! am I left alone on earth
To mourn—I dare not curse—the day
That saw my solitary birth?
Oh! thou wilt love me now no more!
My sinking heart foreboded ill;
But know me all I was before,
Thy sister—friend—Zuleika still.
Thou led'st me here perchance to kill;
If thou hast cause for vengeance, see!
My breast is offered—take thy fill!
Far better with the dead to be
Than live thus nothing now to thee:
Perhaps far worse, for now I know
Why Giaffir always seemed thy foe;
And I, alas! am Giaffir's child,
For whom thou wert contemned, reviled.
If not thy sister—would'st thou save
My life—Oh! bid me be thy slave!"

XII.

"My slave, Zuleika!—nay, I'm thine:
But, gentle love, this transport calm,
Thy lot shall yet be linked with mine;
I swear it by our Prophet's shrine,
And be that thought thy sorrow's balm.
So may the Koran verse displayed
Upon its steel direct my blade,
In danger's hour to guard us both,
As I preserve that awful oath!
The name in which thy heart hath prided
Must change; but, my Zuleika, know,
That tie is widened, not divided,
Although thy Sire's my deadliest foe.
My father was to Giaffir all
That Selim late was deemed to thee;
That brother wrought a brother's fall,

But spared, at least, my infancy!
And lulled me with a vain deceit
That yet a like return may meet.
He reared me, not with tender help,
But like the nephew of a Cain;
He watched me like a lion's whelp,
That gnaws and yet may break his chain.
My father's blood in every vein
Is boiling! but for thy dear sake
No present vengeance will I take;
Though here I must no more remain.
But first, beloved Zuleika! hear
How Giaffir wrought this deed of fear.

XIII.

"How first their strife to rancour grew,
If Love or Envy made them foes,
It matters little if I knew;
In fiery spirits, slights, though few
And thoughtless, will disturb repose.
In war Abdallah's arm was strong,
Remembered yet in Bosniac song,
And Paswan's rebel hordes attest
How little love they bore such guest:
His death is all I need relate,
The stern effect of Giaffir's hate;
And how my birth disclosed to me,
Whate'er beside it makes, hath made me free.

XIV.

"When Paswan, after years of strife,
At last for power, but first for life,
In Widdin's walls too proudly sate,
Our Pachas rallied round the state;
Not last nor least in high command,
Each brother led a separate band;
They gave their Horse-tails to the wind,
And mustering in Sophia's plain
Their tents were pitched, their post assigned;
To one, alas! assigned in vain!
What need of words? the deadly bowl,
By Giaffir's order drugged and given,
With venom subtle as his soul,
Dismissed Abdallah's hence to heaven.
Reclined and feverish in the bath,
He, when the hunter's sport was up,
But little deemed a brother's wrath

To quench his thirst had such a cup:
The bowl a bribed attendant bore;
He drank one draught, nor needed more!
If thou my tale, Zuleika, doubt,
Call Haroun—he can tell it out.

XV.

"The deed once done, and Paswan's feud
In part suppressed, though ne'er subdued,
Abdallah's Pachalick was gained:—
Thou know'st not what in our Divan
Can wealth procure for worse than man—
Abdallah's honours were obtained
By him a brother's murder stained;
'Tis true, the purchase nearly drained
His ill-got treasure, soon replaced.
Would'st question whence? Survey the waste,
And ask the squalid peasant how
His gains repay his broiling brow!—
Why me the stern Usurper spared,
Why thus with me his palace spared,
I know not. Shame—regret—remorse—
And little fear from infant's force—
Besides, adoption as a son
By him whom Heaven accorded none,
Or some unknown cabal, caprice,
Preserved me thus:—but not in peace:
He cannot curb his haughty mood,
Nor I forgive a father's blood.

XVI.

"Within thy Father's house are foes;
Not all who break his bread are true:
To these should I my birth disclose,
His days-his very hours were few:
They only want a heart to lead,
A hand to point them to the deed.
But Haroun only knows, or knew
This tale, whose close is almost nigh:
He in Abdallah's palace grew,
And held that post in his Serai
Which holds he here—he saw him die;
But what could single slavery do?
Avenge his lord? alas! too late;
Or save his son from such a fate?
He chose the last, and when elate
With foes subdued, or friends betrayed,

Proud Giaffir in high triumph sate,
He led me helpless to his gate,
And not in vain it seems essayed
To save the life for which he prayed.
The knowledge of my birth secured
From all and each, but most from me;
Thus Giaffir's safety was ensured.
Removed he too from Roumelie
To this our Asiatic side,
Far from our seats by Danube's tide,
With none but Haroun, who retains
Such knowledge—and that Nubian feels
A Tyrant's secrets are but chains,
From which the captive gladly steals,
And this and more to me reveals:
Such still to guilt just Allah sends—
Slaves, tools, accomplices—no friends!

XVII.

"All this, Zuleika, harshly sounds;
But harsher still my tale must be:
Howe'er my tongue thy softness wounds,
Yet I must prove all truth to thee."
I saw thee start this garb to see,
Yet is it one I oft have worn,
And long must wear: this Galiongée,
To whom thy plighted vow is sworn,
Is leader of those pirate hordes,
Whose laws and lives are on their swords;
To hear whose desolating tale
Would make thy waning cheek more pale:
Those arms thou see'st my band have brought,
The hands that wield are not remote;
This cup too for the rugged knaves
Is filled—once quaffed, they ne'er repine:
Our Prophet might forgive the slaves;
They're only infidels in wine.

XVIII.

"What could I be? Proscribed at home,
And taunted to a wish to roam;
And listless left—for Giaffir's fear
Denied the courser and the spear—
Though oft—Oh, Mahomet! how oft!—
In full Divan the despot scoffed,
As if my weak unwilling hand
Refused the bridle or the brand:

He ever went to war alone,
And pent me here untried—unknown;
To Haroun's care with women left,
By hope unblest, of fame bereft,
While thou—whose softness long endeared,
Though it unmanned me, still had cheered—
To Brusa's walls for safety sent,
Awaited'st there the field's event.
Haroun who saw my spirit pining
Beneath inaction's sluggish yoke,
His captive, though with dread resigning,
My thraldom for a season broke,
On promise to return before
The day when Giaffir's charge was o'er.
'Tis vain—my tongue can not impart
My almost drunkenness of heart,
When first this liberated eye
Surveyed Earth—Ocean—Sun—and Sky—
As if my Spirit pierced them through,
And all their inmost wonders knew!
One word alone can paint to thee
That more than feeling—I was Free!
E'en for thy presence ceased to pine;
The World—nay, Heaven itself was mine!

XIX.

"The shallop of a trusty Moor
Conveyed me from this idle shore;
I longed to see the isles that gem
Old Ocean's purple diadem:
I sought by turns, and saw them all;
But when and where I joined the crew,
With whom I'm pledged to rise or fall,
When all that we design to do
Is done,'twill then be time more meet
To tell thee, when the tale's complete.

XX.

"'Tis true, they are a lawless brood,
But rough in form, nor mild in mood;
And every creed, and every race,
With them hath found—may find a place:
But open speech, and ready hand,
Obedience to their Chief's command;
A soul for every enterprise,
That never sees with Terror's eyes;
Friendship for each, and faith to all,

And vengeance vowed for those who fall,
Have made them fitting instruments
For more than e'en my own intents.
And some—and I have studied all
Distinguished from the vulgar rank,
But chiefly to my council call
The wisdom of the cautious Frank:—
And some to higher thoughts aspire.
The last of Lambro's patriots there
Anticipated freedom share;
And oft around the cavern fire
On visionary schemes debate,
To snatch the Rayahs from their fate.
So let them ease their hearts with prate
Of equal rights, which man ne'er knew;
I have a love for freedom too.
Aye! let me like the ocean-Patriarch roam,
Or only know on land the Tartar's home!
My tent on shore, my galley on the sea,
Are more than cities and Serais to me:
Borne by my steed, or wafted by my sail,
Across the desert, or before the gale,
Bound where thou wilt, my barb! or glide, my prow!
But be the Star that guides the wanderer, Thou!
Thou, my Zuleika, share and bless my bark;
The Dove of peace and promise to mine ark!
Or, since that hope denied in worlds of strife,
Be thou the rainbow to the storms of life!
The evening beam that smiles the clouds away,
And tints to-morrow with prophetic ray!
Blest—as the Muezzin's strain from Mecca's wall
To pilgrims pure and prostrate at his call;
Soft—as the melody of youthful days,
That steals the trembling tear of speechless praise;
Dear—as his native song to Exile's ears,
Shall sound each tone thy long-loved voice endears.
For thee in those bright isles is built a bower
Blooming as Aden in its earliest hour.
A thousand swords, with Selim's heart and hand,
Wait—wave—defend—destroy—at thy command!
Girt by my band, Zuleika at my side,
The spoil of nations shall bedeck my bride.
The Haram's languid years of listless ease
Are well resigned for cares—for joys like these:
Not blind to Fate, I see, where'er I rove,
Unnumbered perils,—but one only love!
Yet well my toils shall that fond breast repay,
Though Fortune frown, or falser friends betray.
How dear the dream in darkest hours of ill,
Should all be changed, to find thee faithful still!
Be but thy soul, like Selim's firmly shown;

To thee be Selim's tender as thine own;
To soothe each sorrow, share in each delight,
Blend every thought, do all—but disunite!
Once free, 'tis mine our horde again to guide;
Friends to each other, foes to aught beside:
Yet there we follow but the bent assigned
By fatal Nature to man's warring kind:
Mark! where his carnage and his conquests cease!
He makes a solitude, and calls it—peace!
I like the rest must use my skill or strength,
But ask no land beyond my sabre's length:
Power sways but by division—her resource
The blest alternative of fraud or force!
Ours be the last; in time Deceit may come
When cities cage us in a social home:
There ev'n thy soul might err—how oft the heart
Corruption shakes which Peril could not part!
And Woman, more than Man, when Death or Woe,
Or even Disgrace, would lay her lover low,
Sunk in the lap of Luxury will shame—
Away suspicion!—not Zuleika's name!
But life is hazard at the best; and here
No more remains to win, and much to fear:
Yes, fear!—the doubt, the dread of losing thee,
By Osman's power, and Giaffir's stern decree.
That dread shall vanish with the favouring gale,
Which Love to-night hath promised to my sail:
No danger daunts the pair his smile hath blest,
Their steps still roving, but their hearts at rest.
With thee all toils are sweet, each clime hath charms;
Earth—sea alike—our world within our arms!
Aye—let the loud winds whistle o'er the deck,
So that those arms cling closer round my neck:
The deepest murmur of this lip shall be,
No sigh for safety, but a prayer for thee!
The war of elements no fears impart
To Love, whose deadliest bane is human Art:
There lie the only rocks our course can check;
Here moments menace—there are years of wreck!
But hence ye thoughts that rise in Horror's shape!
This hour bestows, or ever bars escape.
Few words remain of mine my tale to close;
Of thine but one to waft us from our foes;
Yea—foes—to me will Giaffir's hate decline?
And is not Osman, who would part us, thine?

XXI.

"His head and faith from doubt and death
Returned in time my guard to save;

Few heard, none told, that o'er the wave
From isle to isle I roved the while:
And since, though parted from my band
Too seldom now I leave the land,
No deed they've done, nor deed shall do,
Ere I have heard and doomed it too:
I form the plan—decree the spoil—
Tis fit I oftener share the toil.
But now too long I've held thine ear;
Time presses—floats my bark—and here
We leave behind but hate and fear.
To-morrow Osman with his train
Arrives—to-night must break thy chain:
And would'st thou save that haughty Bey,—
Perchance his life who gave thee thine,—
With me this hour away—away!
But yet, though thou art plighted mine,
Would'st thou recall thy willing vow,
Appalled by truths imparted now,
Here rest I—not to see thee wed:
But be that peril on my head!"

XXII.

Zuleika, mute and motionless,
Stood like that Statue of Distress,
When, her last hope for ever gone,
The Mother hardened into stone;
All in the maid that eye could see
Was but a younger Niobé.
But ere her lip, or even her eye,
Essayed to speak, or look reply,
Beneath the garden's wicket porch
Far flashed on high a blazing torch!
Another—and another—and another—
"Oh! fly—no more—yet now my more than brother!"
Far, wide, through every thicket spread
The fearful lights are gleaming red;
Nor these alone—for each right hand
Is ready with a sheathless brand.
They part—pursue—return, and wheel
With searching flambeau, shining steel;
And last of all, his sabre waving,
Stern Giaffir in his fury raving:
And now almost they touch the cave—
Oh! must that grot be Selim's grave?

XXIII.

Dauntless he stood—"'Tis come—soon past—
One kiss, Zuleika—'tis my last:
But yet my band not far from shore
May hear this signal, see the flash;
Yet now too few—the attempt were rash:
No matter—yet one effort more."
Forth to the cavern mouth he stept;
His pistol's echo rang on high,
Zuleika started not, nor wept,
Despair benumbed her breast and eye!—
"They hear me not, or if they ply
Their oars,'tis but to see me die;
That sound hath drawn my foes more nigh.
Then forth my father's scimitar,
Thou ne'er hast seen less equal war!
Farewell, Zuleika!—Sweet! retire:
Yet stay within—here linger safe,
At thee his rage will only chafe.
Stir not—lest even to thee perchance
Some erring blade or ball should glance.
Fear'st them for him?—may I expire
If in this strife I seek thy sire!
No—though by him that poison poured;
No—though again he call me coward!
But tamely shall I meet their steel?
No—as each crest save his may feel!"

XXIV.

One bound he made, and gained the sand:
Already at his feet hath sunk
The foremost of the prying band,
A gasping head, a quivering trunk:
Another falls—but round him close
A swarming circle of his foes;
From right to left his path he cleft,
And almost met the meeting wave:
His boat appears—not five oars' length—
His comrades strain with desperate strength—
Oh! are they yet in time to save?
His feet the foremost breakers lave;
His band are plunging in the bay,
Their sabres glitter through the spray;
Wet—wild—unwearied to the strand
They struggle—now they touch the land!
They come—'tis but to add to slaughter—
His heart's best blood is on the water.

XXV.

Escaped from shot, unharmed by steel,
Or scarcely grazed its force to feel,
Had Selim won, betrayed, beset,
To where the strand and billows met;
There as his last step left the land,
And the last death-blow dealt his hand—
Ah! wherefore did he turn to look
For her his eye but sought in vain?
That pause, that fatal gaze he took,
Hath doomed his death, or fixed his chain.
Sad proof, in peril and in pain,
How late will Lover's hope remain!
His back was to the dashing spray;
Behind, but close, his comrades lay,
When, at the instant, hissed the ball—
"So may the foes of Giaffir fall!"
Whose voice is heard? whose carbine rang?
Whose bullet through the night-air sang,
Too nearly, deadly aimed to err?
'Tis thine—Abdallah's Murderer!
The father slowly rued thy hate,
The son hath found a quicker fate:
Fast from his breast the blood is bubbling,
The whiteness of the sea-foam troubling—
If aught his lips essayed to groan,
The rushing billows choked the tone!

XXVI.

Morn slowly rolls the clouds away;
Few trophies of the fight are there:
The shouts that shook the midnight-bay
Are silent; but some signs of fray
That strand of strife may bear,
And fragments of each shivered brand;
Steps stamped; and dashed into the sand
The print of many a struggling hand
May there be marked; nor far remote
A broken torch, an oarless boat;
And tangled on the weeds that heap
The beach where shelving to the deep
There lies a white capote!
'Tis rent in twain—one dark-red stain
The wave yet ripples o'er in vain:
But where is he who wore?
Ye! who would o'er his relics weep,
Go, seek them where the surges sweep
Their burthen round Sigæum's steep
And cast on Lemnos' shore:

The sea-birds shriek above the prey,
O'er which their hungry beaks delay,
As shaken on his restless pillow,
His head heaves with the heaving billow;
That hand, whose motion is not life,
Yet feebly seems to menace strife,
Flung by the tossing tide on high,
Then levelled with the wave—
What recks it, though that corse shall lie
Within a living grave?
The bird that tears that prostrate form
Hath only robbed the meaner worm;
The only heart, the only eye
Had bled or wept to see him die,
Had seen those scattered limbs composed,
And mourned above his turban-stone,
That heart hath burst—that eye was closed—
Yea—closed before his own!

XXVII.

By Helle's stream there is a voice of wail!
And Woman's eye is wet—Man's cheek is pale:
Zuleika! last of Giaffir's race,
Thy destined lord is come too late:
He sees not—ne'er shall see thy face!
Can he not hear
The loud Wul-wulleh warn his distant ear?
Thy handmaids weeping at the gate,
The Koran-chanters of the Hymn of Fate,
The silent slaves with folded arms that wait,
Sighs in the hall, and shrieks upon the gale,
Tell him thy tale!
Thou didst not view thy Selim fall!
That fearful moment when he left the cave
Thy heart grew chill:
He was thy hope—thy joy—thy love—thine all,
And that last thought on him thou could'st not save
Sufficed to kill;
Burst forth in one wild cry—and all was still.
Peace to thy broken heart—and virgin grave!
Ah! happy! but of life to lose the worst!
That grief—though deep—though fatal—was thy first!
Thrice happy! ne'er to feel nor fear the force
Of absence—shame—pride—hate—revenge—remorse!
And, oh! that pang where more than Madness lies
The Worm that will not sleep—and never dies;
Thought of the gloomy day and ghastly night,
That dreads the darkness, and yet loathes the light,
That winds around, and tears the quivering heart!

Ah! wherefore not consume it—and depart!
Woe to thee, rash and unrelenting Chief!
Vainly thou heap'st the dust upon thy head,
Vainly the sackcloth o'er thy limbs dost spread:
By that same hand Abdallah—Selim bled.
Now let it tear thy beard in idle grief:
Thy pride of heart, thy bride for Osman's bed,
She, whom thy Sultan had but seen to wed,
Thy Daughter's dead!
Hope of thine age, thy twilight's lonely beam,
The Star hath set that shone on Helle's stream.
What quenched its ray?—the blood that thou hast shed!
Hark! to the hurried question of Despair:
"Where is my child?"—an Echo answers—"Where?"

XXVIII.

Within the place of thousand tombs
That shine beneath, while dark above
The sad but living cypress glooms
And withers not, though branch and leaf
Are stamped with an eternal grief,
Like early unrequited Love,
One spot exists, which ever blooms,
Ev'n in that deadly grove—
A single rose is shedding there
Its lonely lustre, meek and pale:
It looks as planted by Despair—
So white—so faint—the slightest gale
Might whirl the leaves on high;
And yet, though storms and blight assail,
And hands more rude than wintry sky
May wring it from the stem—in vain—
To-morrow sees it bloom again!
The stalk some Spirit gently rears,
And waters with celestial tears;
For well may maids of Helle deem
That this can be no earthly flower,
Which mocks the tempest's withering hour,
And buds unsheltered by a bower;
Nor droops, though Spring refuse her shower,
Nor woos the Summer beam:
To it the livelong night there sings
A Bird unseen—but not remote:
Invisible his airy wings,
But soft as harp that Houri strings
His long entrancing note!
It were the Bulbul; but his throat,
Though mournful, pours not such a strain:
For they who listen cannot leave

The spot, but linger there and grieve,
As if they loved in vain!
And yet so sweet the tears they shed,
'Tis sorrow so unmixed with dread,
They scarce can bear the morn to break
That melancholy spell,
And longer yet would weep and wake,
He sings so wild and well!
But when the day-blush bursts from high
Expires that magic melody.
And some have been who could believe,
(So fondly youthful dreams deceive,
Yet harsh be they that blame,)
That note so piercing and profound
Will shape and syllable its sound
Into Zuleika's name.
'Tis from her cypress summit heard,
That melts in air the liquid word:
'Tis from her lowly virgin earth
That white rose takes its tender birth.
There late was laid a marble stone;
Eve saw it placed—the Morrow gone!
It was no mortal arm that bore
That deep fixed pillar to the shore;
For there, as Helle's legends tell,
Next morn 'twas found where Selim fell;
Lashed by the tumbling tide, whose wave
Denied his bones a holier grave:
And there by night, reclined, 'tis said.
Is seen a ghastly turbaned head:
And hence extended by the billow,
'Tis named the "Pirate-phantom's pillow!"
Where first it lay that mourning flower
Hath flourished; flourisheth this hour,
Alone and dewy—coldly pure and pale;
As weeping Beauty's cheek at Sorrow's tale!

NOTE TO THE MSS. OF THE BRIDE OF ABYDOS

The MSS. of the Bride of Abydos are contained in a bound volume, and in two packets of loose sheets, numbering thirty-two in all, of which eighteen represent additions, etc., to the First Canto; and fourteen additions, etc., to the Second Canto.

The bound volume consists of a rough copy and a fair copy of the first draft of the Bride; the fair copy beginning with the sixth stanza of Canto I.

The "additions" in the bound volume consist of—

1. Stanza xxviii. of Canto II.—here called "Conclusion" (fifty-eight lines). And note on "Sir Orford's Letters."

2. Eight lines beginning, "Eve saw it placed," at the end of stanza xxviii.

3. An emendation of six lines to stanza v. of Canto II., with reference to the comboloio, the Turkish rosary.

4. Forty additional lines to stanza xx. of Canto II., beginning, "For thee in those bright isles," and being the first draft of the addition as printed in the Revises of November 13, etc.

5. Stanza xxvii. of Canto II., twenty-eight lines.

6. Ten additional lines to stanza xxvii., "Ah! happy!"—"depart."

7. Affixed to the rough Copy in stanza xxviii., fifty-eight lines, here called "Continuation." This is the rough Copy of No. 1.

The eighteen loose sheets of additions to Canto I. consist of—

1. The Dedication.

2. Two revisions of "Know ye the land."

3. Seven sheets, Canto I. stanzas i.-v., being the commencement of the Fair Copy in the bound volume.

4. Two sheets of the additional twelve lines to Canto I. stanza vi., "Who hath not proved,"—"Soul."

5. Four sheets of notes to Canto I. stanza vi., dated November 20, November 22, 1813.

6. Two sheets of notes to stanza xvi.

7. Sixteen additional lines to stanza xiii.

The fourteen additional sheets to Canto II. consist of—

1. Ten lines of stanza iv., and four lines of stanza xvii.

2. Two lines and note of stanza v.

3. Sheets of additions, etc., to stanza xx. (eight sheets).

(α) Eight lines, "Or, since that hope,"—"thy command."

(β) "For thee in those bright isles" (twenty-four lines).

(γ) "For thee," etc. (thirty-six lines).

(δ) "Blest as the call" (three variants).

(ε) "For thee in those bright isles" (seven lines).

(ζ) Fourteen lines, "There ev'n thy soul,"—"Zuleika's name," "Aye—let the loud winds,"—"bars escape," additional to stanza xx.

4. Two sheets of five variants of "Ah! wherefore did he turn to look?" being six additional lines to stanza xxv.

5. Thirty-five lines of stanza xxvi.

6. Ten lines, "Ah! happy! but,"—"depart." And eleven lines, "Woe to thee, rash,"—"hast shed," being a continuous addition to stanza xxvii.

REVISES

Endorsed—
i. November 13, 1813.
ii. November 15, 1813.
iii. November 16, 1813.
iv. November 18, 1813.
v. November 19, 1813.
vi. November 21, 1813.
vii. November 23, 1813.
viii. November 24, 1813. A wrong date,
ix. November 25, 1813.
x. An imperfect revise = Nos. i.-v.

Lord Byron – A Short Biography

Byron, one of England's greatest poets, endured a quite difficult background. His father, Captain John "Mad Jack" Byron had married his second wife, the former Catherine Gordon, a descendant of Cardinal Beaton and heiress of the Gight estate in Aberdeenshire, Scotland for the same reason that he married his first: her money. Byron's mother-to-be had to sell her land and title to pay her new husband's debts and within two years the large estate of £23,500, had been squandered, leaving her with an annual income in trust of £150. In a move to avoid his creditors, Catherine accompanied her husband to France in 1786, but returned to England at the end of 1787 in order to give birth to her son on English soil.

George Gordon Byron was born on January 22nd 1788, in lodgings, at Holles Street in London although there is a conflicting account of him having been born in Dover.

He was christened, at St Marylebone Parish Church, George Gordon Byron, after his maternal grandfather, George Gordon of Gight, a descendant of James I of Scotland, who, in 1779, had committed suicide.

In 1790 Catherine moved back to Aberdeenshire and it was here that Byron spent his childhood. His father joined them in their lodgings in Queen Street, but the couple quickly separated. Catherine was prone to mood swings and melancholy. Her husband continued to borrow money from her and she fell deeper into debt. It was one of these "loans" that allowed him to travel to Valenciennes, France, where he died in 1791.

When Byron's great-uncle, the "wicked" Lord Byron, died on 21 May 1798, the 10-year-old boy became the 6th Baron Byron of Rochdale and inherited the ancestral home, Newstead Abbey, in Nottinghamshire. However the Abbey was in a state of disrepair and it was leased to Lord Grey de Ruthyn, and others for several years.

Catherine's parenting swung between either spoiling or indulging her son to stubbornly refusing every plea. Her drinking disgusted him, and he mocked her short and corpulent frame. She did retaliate and, in a fit of temper, once called him as "a lame brat", on account of his club-foot, an issue on which we was very sensitive. He referred to himself as "le diable boiteux" ("the limping devil").

Byron early education was taken at Aberdeen Grammar School, and in August 1799 he entered the school of Dr. William Glennie, in Dulwich. He was encouraged to exercise in moderation but could not restrain himself from "violent" bouts in an attempt to overcompensate for his deformed foot. His mother interfered, often withdrawing him from school, and resulting in him lacking discipline and neglecting his classical studies.

In 1801 he was sent to Harrow, where he remained until July 1805. Byron was an excellent orator but undistinguished student and an unskilled cricketer but strangely he did represent the school in the very first Eton v Harrow cricket match at Lord's in 1805.

Byron, always prone to over-indulge, fell in love with Mary Chaworth, whom he met while at school, and thence refused to return to Harrow in September 1803. His mother wrote, "He has no indisposition that I know of but love, desperate love, the worst of all maladies in my opinion. In short, the boy is distractedly in love with Miss Chaworth."

He did finally return in January 1804, and described his friends there; "My school friendships were with me passions for I was always violent." His nostalgic poems about his Harrow friendships, in his book Childish Recollections, published in 1806, talk of a "consciousness of sexual differences that may in the end make England untenable to him".

The following autumn he attended Trinity College, Cambridge, where he met and formed a close bond with John Edleston. On his "protégé" Byron wrote, "He has been my almost constant associate since October, 1805, when I entered Trinity College. His voice first attracted my attention, his countenance fixed it, and his manners attached me to him forever." In his memory Byron composed Thyrza, a series of elegies. In later years Byron described the affair as "a violent, though pure love and passion". The public were beginning to view homosexuality with increasing distaste and the law now specified such sanctions as public hanging against convicted or even suspected offenders. Though equally Byron may just be using 'pure' out of respect for Edleston's innocence, in contrast to the more sexually overt relations experienced at Harrow School. Byron is now thought of as bi-sexual though more fulfilled, on all levels, by women.

While not at school or college, Byron lived with his mother in Southwell, Nottinghamshire. While there, he cultivated friendships with Elizabeth Pigot and her brother, John, with whom he staged two plays for the entertainment of the local community. During this time, with the help of Elizabeth, who copied his rough drafts, he wrote his first volumes of poetry, Fugitive Pieces, which included poems written when Byron was only 14. However, it was promptly recalled and burned on the advice of his friend, the Reverend J. T. Becher, on account of its more amorous verses, particularly the poem To Mary.

Hours of Idleness, which collected many of the previous poems, along with recent compositions, was the culminating book. The savage, anonymous criticism this received in the Edinburgh Review prompted his first major satire, English Bards and Scotch Reviewers in 1809. This was put into the hands of his relative, R. C. Dallas, requesting him to "...get it published without his name". Although published anonymously Byron was generally known to be the author. The work so upset some of his critics they challenged Byron to a duel. Of course, over time, it became a mark of renown to be the target of Byron's pen.

Byron first took his seat in the House of Lords March 13th, 1809. He was a strong advocate of social reform, and one of the few Parliamentary defenders of the Luddites: specifically, he was against a death penalty for Luddite "frame breakers" in Nottinghamshire, who destroyed the textile machines that were putting them out of work. His first speech before the Lords, on February 27th, 1812, sarcastically referenced the "benefits" of automation, which he saw as producing inferior material as well as putting people out of work, and concluded the proposed law was only missing two things to be effective: "Twelve Butchers for a Jury and a Jeffries for a Judge!"

Two months later, Byron made another impassioned speech before the House in support of Catholic emancipation. He expressed opposition to the established religion because it was unfair to people who practiced other faiths.

Out of this period would follow several overtly political poems; Song for the Luddites (1816), The Landlords' Interest, Canto XIV of The Age of Bronze, Wellington: The Best of the Cut-Throats (1819) and The Intellectual Eunuch Castlereagh (1818).

Like his father Byron racked up numerous debts. His mother thought he had "reckless disregard for money" and lived in fear of her son's creditors.

Between1809 to 1811, Byron went on the Grand Tour, then customary for a young nobleman. The Napoleonic Wars meant most of Europe had to be avoided, and he instead ventured south to the Mediterranean.

There is some correspondence among his circle of Cambridge friends that suggests that another motive was the hope of homosexual experience, and other theories saying that he was worried about a possible dalliance with a married woman, Mary Chaworth, his former love.

But other possibilities exist. Byron had read much about the Ottoman and Persian lands as a child, was attracted to Islam (especially Sufi mysticism), and later wrote, "With these countries, and events connected with them, all my really poetical feelings begin and end."

Byron began his trip in Portugal from where he wrote a letter to his friend Mr. Hodgson in which he describes his mastery of the Portuguese language, consisting mainly of swearing and insults. Byron particularly enjoyed his stay in Sintra that is described in Childe Harold's Pilgrimage as "glorious Eden". From Lisbon he travelled overland to Seville, Jerez de la Frontera, Cádiz, Gibraltar and from there by sea on to Malta and Greece.

While in Athens, Byron met 14-year-old Nicolò Giraud, who became quite close and taught him Italian. Byron sent Giraud to school at a monastery in Malta and in his will, though later taken out, bequeathed him a sizeable sum.

Byron then moved on to Smyrna, and then Constantinople on board HMS Salsette. While HMS Salsette was anchored awaiting Ottoman permission to dock at the city, on May 3rd, 1810 Byron and Lieutenant Ekenhead, of Salsette 's Marines, swam the Hellespont. Byron commemorated this feat in the second canto of Don Juan.

When he sailed back to England in April 1811, he travelled, for a time, aboard the transport ship Hydra, which had on board the last large shipments of Lord Elgin's marbles, a piece of vandalism that Byron had longed railed against. The last leg of his voyage home was from Malta in aboard HMS Volage. He arrived at Sheerness, Kent, on July 14th. He was home after two years away.

On August 2nd, his mother died. "I had but one friend in the world," he exclaimed, "and she is gone."

The following year, 1812, Byron became a sensation with the publication, via his literary agent and family relative R. C. Dallas, of the first two cantos of 'Childe Harold's Pilgrimage'. He rapidly became the most brilliant star in the dazzling world of Regency London, sought after at every society venue, elected to several exclusive clubs, and frequented the most fashionable London drawing-rooms. His own words recall; "I awoke one morning and found myself famous". The Edinburgh Review allowed that Byron had "improved marvellously since his last appearance at our tribunal." He followed up his success with the poem's last two cantos, as well as four equally celebrated "Oriental Tales": The Giaour, The Bride of Abydos, The Corsair and Lara.

His affair with Lady Caroline Lamb (who called him "mad, bad and dangerous to know"), as well as other women and the constant pressure of debt, caused him to seek a suitable marriage i.e. marry wealth. One choice was Annabella Milbanke. But in 1813 he met again, after four years, his half-sister, Augusta Leigh. Rumours of incest constantly surrounded the pair; Augusta, who was married, gave birth on April 15th, 1814 to her third daughter, Elizabeth Medora Leigh, and Byron is suspected to be the father.

To escape from debts and rumours he now sought, in earnest, to marry Annabella, (said to be the likely heiress of a rich uncle). They married on January 2nd, 1815, and their daughter, Ada, was born in December of that year. However Byron's continuing obsession with Augusta and dalliances with others made their marriage a misery.

Annabella thought Byron insane and she left him, taking Ada, in January 1816 and began proceedings for a legal separation. For Byron the scandal of the separation, the continuing rumours about Augusta, and ever-increasing debts were to now force him to leave England.

He passed through Belgium and along the river Rhine and by the summer was settled at the Villa Diodati by Lake Geneva, Switzerland, with his personal physician, the young, brilliant, and handsome John William Polidori. There Byron befriended the poet Percy Bysshe Shelley, and his future wife Mary Godwin. He was also joined by Mary's stepsister, Claire Clairmont, with whom, almost inevitably, he had had an affair with in London.

Kept indoors at the Villa Diodati by the incessant rain during three days in June, the five turned to writing. Mary Shelley produced what would become Frankenstein, or The Modern Prometheus, and Polidori was inspired by a fragmentary story of Byron's, Fragment of a Novel, to produce The Vampyre, the progenitor of the romantic vampire genre.

Byron's story fragment was published as a postscript to Mazeppa; he also now wrote the third canto of Childe Harold.

Byron wintered in Venice, pausing his travels when he fell in love with Marianna Segati, in whose Venice house he was lodging, but who was soon replaced by 22-year-old Margarita Cogni; both women were married. Cogni, who could not read or write, left her husband to move into Byron's Venice house. Their fighting often caused Byron to spend nights in his gondola; when he asked her to leave the house, she threw herself into the Venetian canal.

In a visit to San Lazzaro degli Armeni in Venice, he began to immerse himself in Armenian culture. He learned the Armenian language, and attended many seminars about language and history. He co-authored English Grammar and Armenian in 1817, and Armenian Grammar and English in 1819, where he included quotations from classical and modern Armenian and later, in 1821, participated in the compilation of the English Armenian dictionary, and in the preface he mapped out the relationship of the Armenians with, and the oppression of, the Turkish "pashas" and the Persian satraps, and their struggle for liberation.

In 1817 after a visit to Rome and back in Venice, he wrote the fourth canto of Childe Harold and sold his ancestral home, Newstead Abbey, as well as publishing Manfred; A Dramatic Poem and , Cain; A Mystery.

Byron wrote the first five cantos of his renowned Don Juan between 1818 and 1820. And besides work and adventure there was always love. Women, of course, were always in evidence and the young Countess Teresa Guiccioli found her first love in Byron, who in turn asked her to elope with him. They lived in Ravenna between 1819 and 1821 where he continued Don Juan and also wrote the Ravenna Diary, My Dictionary and Recollections.

It was here that he now received visits from Percy Bysshe Shelley and Thomas Moore.

Of Byron's lifestyle in Ravenna Shelley informs us that; "Lord Byron gets up at two. I get up, quite contrary to my usual custom ... at 12. After breakfast we sit talking till six. From six to eight we gallop through the pine forest which divide Ravenna from the sea; we then come home and dine, and sit up gossiping till six in the morning. I don't suppose this will kill me in a week or fortnight, but I shall not try it longer. Lord B.'s establishment consists, besides servants, of ten horses, eight enormous dogs, three monkeys, five cats, an eagle, a crow, and a falcon; and all these, except the horses, walk about the house, which every now and then resounds with their unarbitrated quarrels, as if they were the masters of it... . [P.S.] I find that my enumeration of the animals in this Circean Palace was defective .... I have just met on the grand staircase five peacocks, two guinea hens, and an Egyptian crane. I wonder who all these animals were before they were changed into these shapes."

From 1821 to 1822, he finished Cantos 6–12 of Don Juan at Pisa, and in the same year he joined with Leigh Hunt and Percy Bysshe Shelley in starting a short-lived newspaper, The Liberal, in the first number of which appeared The Vision of Judgment.

For the first time since his arrival in Italy, Byron found himself tempted to give dinner parties; his guests included the Shelleys, Edward Ellerker Williams, Thomas Medwin, John Taaffe and Edward John Trelawney; and "never", as Shelley said, "did he display himself to more advantage than on these occasions; being at once polite and cordial, full of social hilarity and the most perfect good humour; never diverging into ungraceful merriment, and yet keeping up the spirit of liveliness throughout the evening."

Byron's mother-in-law Judith Noel, the Hon. Lady Milbanke, died in 1822. Her will required that he change his surname to "Noel" in order for him to inherit half of her estate. He obtained a Royal Warrant allowing him to "take and use the surname of Noel only". The Royal Warrant also allowed him to "subscribe the said surname of Noel before all titles of honour", and from that point he signed himself "Noel Byron" (the usual signature of a peer being merely the peerage, in this case simply "Byron").

The Shelley's and Williams had rented a house on the coast and had a schooner built. Byron decided that he too should have his own yacht, and engaged Trelawny's friend, Captain Daniel Roberts, to design and construct the boat. It was named the Bolivar.

On July 8th, 1822 Shelley drowned in a boating accident. Byron attended the funeral. Shelley was cremated on the beach at Viareggio where his body had washed up. His ashes were later interred in Rome in the cemetery in Rome where lay already his son William and John Keats.

Byron was living in Genoa when, in 1823, while growing bored, he accepted a call for his help from representatives of the movement for Greek independence from the Ottoman Empire. With the assistance of his banker and Captain Daniel Roberts, Byron chartered the Brig Hercules to take him to Greece. On 16 July, Byron left Genoa arriving at Kefalonia in the Ionian Islands on August 4th.

Byron had spent £4,000 of his own money to refit the Greek fleet and sailed for Missolonghi in western Greece, arriving on December 29th, to join Alexandros Mavrokordatos, a Greek politician with military power. When the famous Danish sculptor Bertel Thorvaldsen heard about Byron's heroics in Greece, he voluntarily re-sculpted his earlier bust of Byron in Greek marble.

Mavrokordatos and Byron planned to attack the Turkish-held fortress of Lepanto, at the mouth of the Gulf of Corinth. Byron employed a fire-master to prepare artillery and took part of the rebel army under his own command, despite his lack of military experience. Before the expedition could sail, on February 15th, 1824, he fell ill, and the usual remedy of bloodletting weakened him further. He made a partial recovery, but in early April he caught a violent cold which further therapeutic bleeding, insisted on by his doctors, aggravated. He developed a violent fever, and died in Missolonghi on April 19th.

Alfred, Lord Tennyson would later recall the shocked reaction in Britain when word was received of Byron's death. The Greeks mourned Lord Byron deeply, and he became a hero. The Greek form of "Byron", continues in popularity as a name in Greece, and a town near Athens is called Vyronas in his honour.

Byron's body was embalmed, but the Greeks wanted their hero to stay with them. Some say his heart was removed to remain in Missolonghi. His body was returned to England (despite his dying wishes that it should not) for burial in Westminster Abbey, but the Abbey refused to accept it on the grounds of "questionable morality".

Huge crowds viewed his body as he lay in state for two days in London before being buried at the Church of St. Mary Magdalene in Hucknall, Nottinghamshire. A marble slab given by the King of Greece is laid directly above Byron's grave.

Byron's friends had raised the sum of £1,000 to commission a statue of the writer by the sculptor Thorvaldsen. However for a decade after the statue was completed, in 1834, most British institutions had refused to accept it, among them the British Museum, St. Paul's Cathedral,

Westminster Abbey and the National Gallery, and it remained in storage. Finally Trinity College, Cambridge, placed the statue in its library.

Finally, in 1969, a145 years after Byron's death, a memorial to him was placed in Westminster Abbey. It had been pointedly noted by the New York Times that "People are beginning to ask whether this ignoring of Byron is not a thing of which England should be ashamed ... a bust or a tablet might be put in the Poets' Corner and England be relieved of ingratitude toward one of her really great sons." At last Byron was where he should be.

Lord Byron – A Concise Bibliography

The Major Works
Hours of Idleness (1807)
English Bards and Scotch Reviewers (1809)
Childe Harold's Pilgrimage, Cantos I & II (1812)
The Giaour (1813)
The Bride of Abydos (1813)
The Corsair (1814)
Lara, A Tale (1814)
Hebrew Melodies (1815)
The Siege of Corinth (1816)
Parisina (1816)
The Prisoner of Chillon (1816)
The Dream (1816)
Prometheus (1816)
Darkness (1816)
Manfred (1817)
The Lament of Tasso (1817)
Beppo (1818)
Childe Harold's Pilgrimage (1818)
Don Juan (1819–1824; incomplete on Byron's death in 1824)
Mazeppa (1819)
The Prophecy of Dante (1819)
Marino Faliero (1820)
Sardanapalus (1821)
The Two Foscari (1821)
Cain (1821)
The Vision of Judgment (1821)
Heaven and Earth (1821)
Werner (1822)
The Age of Bronze (1823)
The Island (1823)
The Deformed Transformed (1824)

Index of Titles (This is an abbreviated, not a complete, list of his poems).
A
Address, spoken at the Opening of Drury-Lane Theatre, Saturday, October 10, 1812

The Adieu
Adieu to the Muse (same as "Farewell to the Muse")
Address intended to be recited at the Caledonian Meeting
Adrian's Address to his Soul when Dying
The Age of Bronze (a transcription project)
"All is Vanity, Saith the Preacher"
And Thou Art Dead, as Young and Fair
And Wilt Thou Weep When I am Low?
Another Simple Ballat
Answer to —'s Professions of Affection
Answer to a Beautiful Poem
Answer to Some Elegant Verses Sent by a Friend to the Author, & etc.
Answer to the Foregoing, Addressed to Miss —
Aristomenes
Away, Away, Ye Notes of Woe!

B

Ballad
Beppo, a Venetian Story
The Blues, a Literary Eclogue
Bowles and Campbell
The Bride of Abydos, a Turkish Tale (A transcription project)
Bright Be the Place of Thy Soul! (see "Stanzas for Music")
By the Rivers of Babylon We Sat Down and Wept
"By the Waters of Babylon"

C

Cain, a Mystery (A transcription project)
The Chain I gave (same as "From the Turkish")
The Charity Ball
Childe Harold's Good Night (from Childe Harold's Pilgrimage, Canto I.)
Childe Harold's Pilgrimage
Childish Recollections
Churchill's Grave
The Conquest
The Cornelian
The Corsair: A Tale
The Curse of Minerva

D

Damætas
Darkness
The Death of Calmar and Orla
The Deformed Transformed, a drama (A transcription project)
The Destruction of Sennacherib
The Devil's Drive
Don Juan
A Dream (same as "Darkness")
The Dream
The Duel

E

E Nihilo Nihil; or, An Epigram Bewitched
Egotism. A Letter to J. T. Becher
Elegiac Stanzas on the Death of Sir Peter Parker, Bart.
Elegy
Elegy on Newstead Abbey
Elegy on the Death of Sir Peter Parker (same "Elegiac Stanzas on the Death of Sir Peter Parker, Bart.")
Endorsement to the Deed of Separation, in the April of 1816
English Bards, and Scotch Reviewers, a Satire
Epigram (If for Silver, or for Gold)
Epigram (In Digging up your Bones, Tom Paine)
Epigram (It Seems That the Braziers Propose Soon to Pass)
Epigram (The world is a bundle of hay)
Epigram on an Old Lady Who Had Some Curious Notions Respecting the Soul
Epigrams (Oh, Castlereagh! Thou Art a Patriot Now)
Epilogue
The Episode of Nisus and Euryalus (A Paraphrase from the Æneid, Lib. 9.)
Epistle from Mr. Murray to Dr. Polidori
Epistle to a Friend
Epistle to Augusta
Epistle to Mr. Murray
Epitaph
Epitaph for Joseph Blacket, Late Poet and Shoemaker
Epitaph for William Pitt
Epitaph on a Beloved Friend
Epitaph on a Friend (same as "Epitaph on a Beloved Friend")
Epitaph on John Adams, of Southwell
Epitaph to a Dog
Euthanasia

F

Fame, Wisdom, Love, and Power Were Mine (same as "All is Vanity, saith the Preacher")
Fare Thee Well
Farewell (same as "Farewell! if Ever Fondest Prayer")
Farewell Petition to J. C. H., Esqre.
Farewell to Malta
Farewell to the Muse
Fill the Goblet Again
The First Kiss of Love
A Fragment (Could I Remount the River of My Years)
Fragment (Hills of Annesley, Bleak and Barren)
A Fragment (When, to Their Airy Hall, my Fathers' Voice)
Fragment from the "Monk of Athos"
Fragment of a Translation from the 9th Book of Virgil's Æneid (compare "The Episode of Nisus and Euryalus")
Fragment of an Epistle to Thomas Moore
Fragments of School Exercises: From the "Prometheus Vinctus" of Æschylus
Francesca of Rimini
Francisca
From Anacreon Ode 3. ('Twas Now the Hour When Night Had Driven)
From Job (same as "A Spirit Passed Before Me")

From the French (Ægle, Beauty and Poet, Has Two Little Crimes)
From the French (Must Thou Go, my Glorious Chief)
From the Last Hill That Looks on Thy Once Holy Dome (same as "On the Day of the Destruction of Jerusalem by Titus")
From the Portuguese
From the Turkish (same as "The Chain I Gave")

G

G. G. B. to E. P. (same as "To M. S. G.") (When I Dream That You Love Me, you'll surely Forgive)
The Giaour
The Girl of Cadiz
Granta. A Medley

H

The Harp the Monarch Minstrel Swept
Heaven and Earth, a Mystery (A transcription project)
Hebrew Melodies
Herod's Lament for Mariamne
Hints from Horace (A transcription project)
Hours of Idleness

I

I Speak Not, I Trace Not, I Breathe Not Thy Name (see "Stanzas for Music")
I Saw Thee Weep
I Would I Were a Careless Child
Ich Dien
If Sometimes in the Haunts of Men
If That High World
Imitated from Catullus
Imitation of Tibullus
Impromptu
Impromptu, in Reply to a Friend
In the Valley of Waters (same as "By the Waters of Babylon")
Inscription on the Monument of a Newfoundland Dog
The Island, or Christian and His Comrades
The Irish Avatar
It is the Hour (compare with first stanza of Parisina)

J

Jeptha's Daughter
John Keats
Journal in Cephalonia
Julian [a Fragment]

K

L

La Revanche
Lachin y Gair
L'Amitié est L'Amour sans Ailes
The Lament of Tasso

Lara: A Tale
Last Words on Greece
Lines Addressed by Lord Byron to Mr. Hobhouse on his Election for Westminster
Lines Addressed to a Young Lady
Lines Addressed to the Rev. J. T. Becher
Lines Inscribed Upon a Cup Formed From a Skull
Lines in the Travellers' Book at Orchomenus
Lines on Hearing That Lady Byron Was Ill
Lines on Sir Peter Parker (same as "Elegiac Stanzas on the Death of Sir Peter Parker, Bart.")
Lines to a Lady Weeping (same as "To a Lady Weeping")
Lines to Mr. Hodgson
Lines Written Beneath a Picture
Lines Written Beneath an Elm in the Churchyard of Harrow
Lines Written in an Album, At Malta
Lines Written in "Letters of an Italian Nun and an English Gentleman
Lines Written on a Blank Leaf of The Pleasures of Memory
Lord Byron's Verses on Sam Rogers
Love and Death
Love and Gold
A Love Song. To — (same as "Remind me not, Remind me not")
Love's Last Adieu
Lucietta. A Fragment

M

Maid of Athens, Ere We Part
Manfred, a Dramatic Poem
Marino Faliero, Doge of Venice, an Historical Tragedy (1821) (A transcription project)
Martial, Lib. I. Epig. I.
Mazeppa
Monody on the Death of the Right Hon. R. B. Sheridan
The Morgante Maggiore (A transcription project)
My Boy Hobbie O
My Epitaph
My Soul is Dark

N

Napoleon's Farewell
Napoleon's Snuff-box
The New Vicar of Bray
Newstead Abbey

O

An Occasional Prologue
Ode from the French
Ode on Venice
Ode to a Lady Whose Lover was Killed by a Ball, Which at the Same Time Shivered a Portrait Next His Heart
Ode to Napoleon Buonaparte
An Ode to the Framers of the Frame Bill
Oh! Snatched Away in Beauty's Bloom
Oh! Weep for Those

On a Change of Masters at a Great Public School
On a Cornelian Heart Which Was Broken
On a Distant View of the Village and School of Harrow on the Hill, 1806
On a Royal Visit to the Vaults (Windsor Poetics)
On Being Asked What Was the "Origin of Love"
On Finding a Fan
On Jordan's Banks
On Leaving Newstead Abbey
On Lord Thurlow's Poems
On Moore's Last Operatic Farce, or Farcical Opera
On My Thirty-third Birthday
On My Wedding-Day
On Napoleon's Escape from Elba
On Parting
On Revisiting Harrow
On Sam Rogers (same as "Lord Byron's Verses on Sam Rogers")
On the Birth of John William Rizzo Hoppner
On the Bust of Helen by Canova
On the Day of the Destruction of Jerusalem by Titus
On the Death of — Thyrza (same as "To Thyrza")
On the Death of a Young Lady
On the Death of Mr. Fox
On the Death of the Duke of Dorset
On the Eyes of Miss A— H—
On the Quotation
On the Star of "the Legion of Honour"
On this Day I complete my Thirty-sixth Year
One Struggle More, and I Am Free
Oscar of Alva
Ossian's Address to the Sun in "Carthon"

P
Parenthetical Address
Parisina
Pignus Amoris
The Prayer of Nature
The Prisoner of Chillon
The Prophecy of Dante, a Poem

Q
Quem Deus Vult Perdere Prius Dementat
Queries to Casuists

R
R. C. Dallas
Remember Him, whom Passion's Power
Remember Thee! Remember thee!
Remembrance
Remind Me Not, Remind Me Not
Reply to Some Verses of J. M. B. Pigot, Esq., on the Cruelty of his Mistress

S

Sardanapalus, a Tragedy (A transcription project)
Saul
She Walks in Beauty
The Siege of Corinth
A Sketch From Life
So We'll Go No More A-Roving
Soliloquy of a Bard in the Country
Sonetto di Vittorelli
Song (Breeze of the Night in Gentler Sighs)
Song (Fill the Goblet Again! For I Never Before)
Song (Maid of Athens, Ere We Part) (same as "Maid of Athens, Ere We Part")
Song (Thou Art Not False, But Thou Art fickle) same as "Thou Art Not False, But Thou Art Fickle")
Song (When I Roved a Young Highlander) (same as "When I Roved a Young Highlander")
Song For the Luddites
Song of Saul Before His Last Battle
Song To the Suliotes
Sonnet On Chillon
Sonnet on the Nuptials of the Marquis Antonio Cavalli with the Countess Clelia Rasponi of Ravenna
Sonnet, to Genevra (Thine eyes' Blue Tenderness, Thy Long Fair Hair)
Sonnet, to Generva (Thy Cheek is Pale with Thought, but Not From Woe). aka "Sonnet, to the Same"
Sonnet to Lake Leman
Sonnet to the Prince Regent
The Spell is Broke, the Charm is Flown!
A Spirit Passed Before Me
Stanzas (And Thou Art Dead, as Young and Fair)
Stanzas (And Wilt Thou Weep When I am Low?) (same as "And Wilt Thou Weep When I Am Low?")
Stanzas (Away, Away, Ye Notes of Woe)
Stanzas (Chill and Mirk is the Nightly Blast) (same as "Stanzas Composed During a Thunderstorm")
Stanzas (Could Love For Ever)
Stanzas (I Would I Were a Careless Child) (same as "I Would I Were a Careless Child")
Stanzas (If Sometimes in the Haunts of Men)
Stanzas (One Struggle More, and I Am Free)
Stanzas (Remember Him, Whom Passion's Power)
Stanzas (Thou Art Not False, but Thou Art Fickle)
Stanzas (Through Cloudless Skies, in Silvery Sheen) (same as "Stanzas Written in Passing the Ambracian Gulf")
Stanzas (When a Man Hath No Freedom to Fight For at Home)
Stanzas Composed During a Thunderstorm
Stanzas For Music (Bright Be the Place of Thy Soul!)
Stanzas For Music (I Speak Not, I Trace Not, I Breathe Not Thy Name)
Stanzas For Music (There Be None of Beauty's Daughters)
Stanzas For Music (There's Not a Joy the World Can Give Like That it Takes Away)
Stanzas For Music (They Say That Hope is Happiness)
Stanzas To — (same as "Stanzas to Augusta": Though the Day of My Destiny's Over)
Stanzas To a Hindoo Air
Stanzas To a Lady, on Leaving England
Stanzas To a Lady, with the Poems of Camoëns
Stanzas To Augusta (When all around grew drear and dark)
Stanzas To Augusta (Though the day of my Destiny's over)
Stanzas To Jessy

Stanzas To the Po
Stanzas To the Same (same as "There was a Time, I need not name")
Stanzas Written in Passing the Ambracian Gulf
Stanzas Written on the Road Between Florence and Pisa
Substitute For an Epitaph
Sun of the Sleepless!
Sympathetic Address to a Young Lady (same as "Lines to a Lady Weeping")

T

The Tear
There Be None of Beauty's Daughters (see "Stanzas for Music")
There Was a Time, I Need Not Name
There's Not a Joy the World Can Give Like That it Takes Away (see "Stanzas for Music")
They say that Hope is Happiness (see "Stanzas for Music")
Thou Art Not False, but Thou Art Fickle
Thou Whose Spell Can Raise the Dead (same as "Saul")
Thoughts Suggested by a College Examination
Thy Days are Done
To — (But Once I Dared to Lift My Eyes)
To — (Oh! Well I Know Your Subtle Sex)
To A— (same as "To M—")
To a Beautiful Quaker
To a Knot of Ungenerous Critics
To a Lady (Oh! Had My Fate Been Join'd with Thine)
To a Lady (This Band, Which Bound Thy yellow Hair)
To a Lady (When Man, Expell'd from Eden's Bowers)
To a Lady Weeping (same as "Lines To a Lady Weeping")
To a Lady who Presented to the Author a Lock of Hair Braided with His Own, and Appointed a Night in December to Meet Him in the Garden
To a Vain Lady
To a Youthful Friend
To an Oak at Newstead
To Anne (Oh, Anne, Your Offences to Me Have Been Grievous)
To Anne (Oh Say Not, Sweet Anne, That the Fates Have Decreed)
To Belshazzar
To Caroline (Oh! When Shall the Grave Hide For Ever My Sorrow?)
To Caroline (Think'st thou I saw thy beauteous eyes)
To Caroline (When I Hear you Express an Affection so Warm)
To Caroline (You Say You Love, and Yet Your Eye)
To D—
To Dives. A Fragment
To E—
To Edward Noel Long, Esq.
To Eliza
To Emma
To E. N. L. Esq. (same as "To Edward Noel Long, Esq.")
To Florence
To George Anson Byron (?)
To George, Earl Delawarr
To Harriet

To Ianthe (The "Origin of Love!"—Ah, why) (same as "On Being Asked What Was the 'Origin of Love'")
To Ianthe (from Canto I of Childe Harold's Pilgrimage) (Not in Those Climes Where I Have Late Been Straying)
To Inez (from Canto I of Childe Harold's Pilgrimage) (Nay, Smile Not at My Sullen Brow)
To Julia (same as "To Lesbia!")
To Lesbia!
To Lord Thurlow
To M—
To Maria — (same as "To Emma")
To Mrs. — (same as "Well! Thou Art Happy")
To Mrs. Musters (same as "Stanzas To a Lady, On Leaving England")
To M. S. G. (When I Dream That You Love Me, You'll Surely Forgive)
To M. S. G. (Whene'er I View Those Lips of Thine)
To Marion
To Mary, on Receiving Her Picture
To Miss E. P. (same as "To Eliza")
To Mr. Murray (For Orford and for Waldegrave)
To Mr. Murray (Strahan, Tonson, Lintot of the Times)
To Mr. Murray (To Hook the Reader, You, John Murray)
To my Son
To Penelope
To Romance
To Samuel Rogers, Esq. (same as "Lines Written On a Blank Leaf of The Pleasures of Memory")
To Sir W. D. (same as "To a Youthful Friend")
To the Author of a Sonnet
To the Countess of Blessington
To the Duke of D— (same as "To the Duke of Dorset")
To the Duke of Dorset
To the Earl of — (same as "To the Earl of Clare")
To the Earl of Clare
To the Honble. Mrs. George Lamb
To the Prince Regent on the Repeal of the Bill of Attainder Against Lord E. Fitzgerald, June, 1819. (same as "Sonnet to the Prince Regent")
To the Rev. J. T. Becher (same as "Lines: Addressed to the Rev. J. T. Becher")
To the Same (same as "And Wilt Thou Weep When I Am Low?")
To the Sighing Strephon
To Thomas Moore (My Boat is on the Shore)
To Thomas Moore (Oh you, Who in all Names Can Tickle the Town)
To Thomas Moore (What Are You Doing Now)
To Thyrza (Without a Stone to Mark the Spot)
To Thyrza (One Struggle More, and I Am Free) (same as "One Struggle More, and I am Free")
To Time
To Woman
Translation from Anacreon Ode 1. (I Wish to Tune My Quivering Lyre)
Translation from Anacreon Ode 5. (Mingle with the Genial Bowl)
Translation from Catullus: Ad Lesbiam
Translation from Catullus: Lugete Veneres Cupidinesque
Translation from Horace
Translation from the "Medea" of Euripides [Ll. 627–660]
Translation from Vittorelli

Translation of a Romaic Love Song
Translation of the Epitaph on Virgil and Tibullus, by Domitius Marsus
Translation of the Famous Greek War Song
Translation of the Nurse's Dole in the Medea of Euripides
Translation of the Romaic Song
The Two Foscari, a Tragedy (A transcription project)

U

V

Venice. A Fragment
Verses Found in a Summer-house at Hales-Owen
Versicles
A Version of Ossian's Address to the Sun
A very Mournful Ballad on the Siege and Conquest of Alhama
Vision of Belshazzar
The Vision of Judgment (A transcription project)
A Volume of Nonsense

W

The Waltz, an Apostrophic Hymn
Warriors and Chiefs! (same as "Song of Saul Before His Last Battle")
We Sate Down and Wept by the Waters of Babel (same as "By the Rivers of Babylon We Sat Down and Wept")
Well! Thou art Happy
Were My Bosom as False as Thou Deem'st It To Be
Werner, or The Inheritance, a Tragedy (A transcription project)
When a Man Hath No Freedom to Fight For at Home (see "Stanzas")
When Coldness Wraps This Suffering Clay
When I Roved a Young Highlander
When We Two Parted
The Wild Gazelle
Windsor Poetics
A Woman's Hair
Written after Swimming from Sestos to Abydos
Written at Athens (same as "The Spell is Broke, the Charm is Flown!")
Written at the Request of a Lady in her Memorandum Book (same as "Lines Written in an Album, At Malta")
Written in an Album (same as "Lines Written in an Album, At Malta")
Written in Mrs. Spencer S.'s— (same as "Lines Written in an Album, At Malta")

www.ingramcontent.com/pod-product-compliance
Lightning Source LLC
Chambersburg PA
CBHW061304040426

42444CB00010B/2503